Scientific and Practical Research
(Anthology) : Part-2

Sobirov Javohir Xayrullayevich

© Sobirov Javohir Xayrullayevich
Scientific and Practical Research *(Anthology)* **: Part-2**
By: Sobirov Javohir Xayrullayevich
Edition: June '2025
Publisher:
Taemeer Publications LLC (Michigan, USA / Hyderabad, India)

ISBN 978-93-6908-968-0

© **Sobirov Javohir Xayrullayevich**

Book	:	Scientific and Practical Research (Anthology) : Part-2
Author/s	:	Sobirov Javohir Xayrullayevich
Publisher	:	Taemeer Publications
Year	:	'2025
Pages	:	50
Title Design	:	*Taemeer Web Design*

SCIENTIFIC AND PRACTICAL RESEARCH IN THE THIRD RENAISSANCE

International Anthology

All rights reserved Copyright ©

Compiled by: Sobirov Javokhir

No part of this publication may be reproduced, distributed or transmitted for commercial purposes in any form or by any means, including recording, copying, or other electronic means, without the written permission of the Publisher.

Kamalova Kadriya Fyodorovna, Namangan Engineering and Construction Institute, Associate Professor
INTERFERENCE OF NATIVE LANGUAGE IN RUSSIAN SPEECH OF STUDENTS – LINGUISTS

Annotationt: The article examines the phenomenon of interference of the native Uzbek language in the oral and written Russian speech of students studying Russian as a foreign language. The typical mistakes and difficulties encountered by Uzbek-speaking students in mastering the Russian language related to differences in phonetics, vocabulary, grammar and syntax of the two languages are analyzed. Special attention is paid to the influence of Uzbek language norms on the formation of Russian speech structures and models. The article also offers methodological recommendations for teachers aimed at reducing the level of interference and facilitating the process of learning the Russian language.

Key words: interference, mutual influence, billing, pronunciation, toponyms, bilingualism, linguistics, semantic errors.

Below is the English translation of the provided text.

Introduction

When teaching a foreign language, one of the most discussed problems is the influence of the native language on the acquisition of another, target language. This influence often leads to deviations from the norms of the target language, known as interference. What is interference? This concept denotes the consequence of one language influencing another, that is, applying the norms of one language to another in written or oral speech. The origin of this expression is Latin: *interferens*, from *inter* – between, and *ferens* – carrying, transferring.

Linguistic interference arises from language contact, which can occur both in "verbal communication between two linguistic communities" and in a learning situation. Uzbek students face difficulties in acquiring the Russian language due to the specific features of its grammatical system and the interfering influence of their native language. This is because Russian and Uzbek belong to different language groups, leading to significant divergences between them.

The Uzbek language is based on the Latin alphabet, while Russian uses Cyrillic. These systemic differences are the main sources of interference, as speakers of the two languages transfer elements from one system to another.

Literature Review

The study of interference in translation and interlingual contacts has been addressed by scholars such as V.V. Alimov (1990s-2000s), who made a significant contribution to the study of translation transformations, including interference (1); V.A. Bogoroditsky (1920s-1940s), who examined phonetic interference in bilingualism (2); Baudouin de Courtenay (1920s-1940s), who investigated the mechanisms of one language's influence on another and highlighted the psychological aspects of interference (3); Uriel Weinreich (1953), who introduced the term "interference" in its modern sense – as the penetration of elements from one language into another in bilingualism, and also defined types of interference: phonetic, morphological, syntactic, and lexical (4); V.A. Vinogradov (1930s-1960s), who analyzed the influence of the translator's native language on the structure of the translated text (5); V.Y. Rozentsveig (1970s-1980s), who considered the influence of the linguistic environment on translation and bilingualism (8); L.V. Shcherba (1910s-1940s), who researched phonetic and grammatical interference in foreign language learning. These scholars laid the foundations for further study of interference and its influence on translation activities (10).

Research Methodology

This study uses a comprehensive approach that includes both qualitative and quantitative analysis of errors made by students when acquiring Russian as a foreign language. The research methodology consists of several stages: participant selection, error analysis, experimental basis, contrastive analysis, and the development of methodological recommendations. Based on the analysis results, recommendations are proposed for teachers, aimed at minimizing interference and optimizing the Russian language learning process. In particular, the emphasis is placed on practical work with phonetic, grammatical, and lexical difficulties characteristic of Uzbek-speaking students.

For quantitative error analysis, a statistical method is used to determine the most common types of interference and their frequency in students' speech.

Russian as an academic subject provides ample opportunities for students' humanitarian training. Since it is compulsory in national schools and universities, it is important to further investigate the quality of bilingualism.

To organize effective Russian language classes, it is advisable to combine aspectual and comprehensive approaches, considering the situation. Teachers often encounter speech interference — negative transfer caused by false correspondences between units of two language systems.

Learning Russian is impossible without considering students' native language, as they often think in it, leading to errors. These errors are especially common among schoolchildren whose native language belongs to a different linguistic system [6,

193]. As L.V. Shcherba noted, the native language cannot be removed from students' minds, and they understand a new word or phenomenon through its equivalent in their native language [9, 427].

The problem of interference manifests itself in phonetics, graphics, grammar, lexis, and syntax. Among Uzbek students learning Russian, errors in stress are most frequently encountered. In Russian, stress can be mobile, while in Uzbek, it is fixed and usually falls on the last syllable, leading to a shift in stress when affixes are added. For example, in Uzbek words such as "ish" (work), "ishchi" (worker), and others, the stress remains on the last syllable, which does not correspond to Russian norms.

Difficulties also arise in pronouncing the vowel sounds o, a, and e when Russian-speaking students perceive them in pre-stressed and post-stressed positions, which often leads to incorrect pronunciation and spelling of words, for example: Tashkent (Тошкент) – Tashkent (Ташкент), Yunusabad (Юнусобод) – Yunusabad (Юнусабад).

Furthermore, Uzbek-speaking students experience difficulties in pronouncing Russian sounds absent in Uzbek, such as [ы], [ш], [щ]. The sound [ы] may be replaced by [и], and [щ] by [ш], affecting the accuracy of speech, for example, the word "mashina" (машина) may sound like "masina" (масина).

Analysis and Results

Phonetic interference occurs when the phonetic systems of diffcrent languages interact, leading to pronunciation errors. For example, Uzbek-speaking students may replace the semi-soft [l] with a hard [л] or a soft [н] with a hard [n]. In Uzbek, stress is fixed, which can lead to errors in Russian words, as in the example "inta i" instead of "sintaksis" (syntax). Phonetic interference also affects the lexical meaning of words, as in the case of the Uzbek "hokim" (mayor), which can be perceived as "lekar'" (healer) in Russian.

Graphic and orthographic interference manifests in writing errors, for example, in words like "1997-yil 12-aprel" instead of "1997 god 12 aprelya" (April 12, 1997). Lexical interference arises when words are borrowed when analogues are absent or inconvenient. For example, using the Uzbek "sevgi" instead of "lyubov'" (love) or Russian words in Uzbek phrases, like "U menya imtihan zavtra" instead of "Menda ertaga imtihon" (I have an exam tomorrow).

Grammatical interference leads to errors in cases, verb tenses, and word order. For example, "Ya idu v biblioteka" (I go to library) instead of "Ya idu v biblioteku" (I go to the library). Errors related to gender are also common, as the Uzbek language has no gender category, which makes it difficult to perceive Russian gender. Syntactic interference manifests in transferring word order from Uzbek, for example, "Ya knigu chitayu" (I book read) instead of "Ya chitayu knigu" (I read a book).

Semantic interference occurs when words are perceived through the meanings of another language, as, for example, the Russian "druzhba" (friendship), which can be understood through the Uzbek "do'stlik," including deeper obligations.

To minimize interference, it is important to carefully organize the learning process, identify problems, and seek solutions. Interference continues to be an important topic of linguistic research and requires further study.

We propose using translation exercises to reduce the influence of the native language and prevent interference. These tasks assume that students first analyze the linguistic material, correlate transcriptional signs with the phonetic system and orthoepy norms, and then proceed to communicative tasks. Students compare transcription, pronunciation, and orthography, recording the results for oral speech, after which they read again, which contributes to improved pronunciation. Such exercises, alternating types of speech activity, are recommended for use at an advanced stage of phonetics study to correct articulatory errors.

For successful acquisition of a second language, especially in speaking, the integration of a conscious approach and constant practice is important. Key recommendations for reducing interference:

1. Conscious study of language differences. Teachers and students should understand the differences in the structure of Uzbek and Russian. Comparative analysis of grammar, vocabulary, and syntax helps identify potential sources of errors and prevent them.

2. Practice in the language environment. To minimize interference, it

developed, with artificial ponds, flowers, and rare trees imported from distant lands, all of which are vividly depicted in the painting.

On the right side of the painting, in front of the madrasa, tall poplar trees are growing, even taller than the building itself. The madrasa is painted in golden hues, with its facade adorned with dark blue patterns. The circular, arched windows are set in sections of the building. Alisher Navoi and Husayn Bayqaro stand in bright silhouettes against the dark green backdrop of the trees. From the madrasa doors, stairs descend toward the pond. Bright light radiates from all directions, and the sky is deep, clear blue, evoking the sensation of hearing music.

Sa'dulla Abdullayev's subsequent work is the portrait of the beloved poet and Sufi, Khoja Ahmad Yasawi. In the painting, Yasawi is depicted against the backdrop of the Mogok Attar in Bukhara. The figure in the artwork is portrayed as a man with good

is important to practice the language in a natural environment. Students who are in a Russian-speaking environment or interact with native speakers will be less susceptible to the influence of their native language.

3. Development of metalinguistic awareness. An important step is the ability of students to be aware of their mistakes and grammatical deviations. This is achieved through feedback from teachers and self-analysis of their own language practice.

To reduce the impact of negative interference and utilize positive interference in subsequent translation work, interference needs to be studied. It should be remembered that it can manifest itself throughout the entire process, from the strongest foreign accent to the accidental use of a word or idiom from another language.

Conclusions

We analyzed the interference of the

native language in the Russian speech of linguistics students, which emphasizes the need to understand the influence of the native language on the learning process. It is important that Russian language instruction is perceived as a comprehensive process, including elements of translation, comparison, and analysis of meanings, which contributes to a deeper understanding of the language and facilitates integration into the Russian-speaking environment.

It is important to note that interference can be both a negative and a positive factor. In the first case, it hinders the correct acquisition of a new language; in the second, it can serve as a basis for creating new linguistic constructions. Key factors contributing to interference are the differences in the grammatical systems and phonetic features of the native language and Russian. To minimize these influences, it is necessary to include special methods in the learning process aimed at recognizing and overcoming interference errors. Teachers should pay attention to the peculiarities of students' native language, as well as the possible difficulties they may encounter in the process of learning Russian.

Thus, interference in Uzbek-Russian bilingualism is a natural process that arises from the contact of two different languages. However, with the right approach to teaching and language practice, its influence can be significantly reduced. It is important to pay attention to linguistic differences and encourage language practice in various social and cultural contexts.

References

1. Alimov V.V. *Interference in Translation.* M., 2005. P.24.
2. Bogoroditsky V.A. *Errors of a German in Russian Speech and a Russian in German Speech.* Scientific and pedagogical collection. IV. — Kazan, 1928, pp. 168—177.
3. Baudouin de Courtenay I.A. *Some General Remarks on Linguistics and Language //* Zvegintsev V. A. History of Linguistics of the XIX-XX Centuries in Essays and Excerpts. - M.: Prosveshchenie, 1964. - P. 263-283.
4. Weinreich U. *Languages in Contact: Findings and Problems /* U. Weinreich; translated from English and commented. 1979. Kyiv, -.48p.
5. Vinogradov V.A. *Norm Stratification, Interference, and Language Teaching.* — In: Linguistic Foundations of Language Teaching.

6. Kamalova, K. F. (2022). *Working with texts on specialty in Russian language classes*. In XVIII Vinogradov Readings (pp. 193-195).

7. Kamalova, K. F. (2022). *Problems of teaching Russian in bilingual conditions*. Journal of new century innovations, 6, 91-100.

8. Rozentsveig V. Yu. *Language Contacts* / V. Yu. Rozentsveig. – L.: Nauka, 1972. – 80 67p.

9. Sakaeva L.R. Baranova A.R. *Methodology of Teaching Foreign Languages: A Textbook*. Kazan: KFU, 2016. 189 p.

10. Shcherba L. V. *Language System and Speech Activity* / L. V. Shcherba. – L.: Nauka, 1974. – 427 p.

INTERPRETATION OF HISTORICAL THEMES IN THE WORKS OF ARTIST SADULLA ABDULLAYEV

Zohira Akhatova Daughter of Akhtam, 3rd-year student of the Department of Art History (Visual and Applied Arts) at the Faculty of Art History and Museum Studies, Kamoliddin Behzod National Institute of Fine Arts and Design.

zohiraaxatova5@gmail.com

+998901267420

Annotation: Sadulla Abdullayev. It includes a comparative analysis of as Alisher Navoi and Husayn Boyqaro in Herat, Layla and Majnun, Saddi Iskandariy,

Hayratul Abror, and Alisher Navoi in Samarkand This article provides an analysis of the historical genre works created by the artist Sadulla his works, such.

Keywords: Color depiction, Artist, Sadulla Abdullayev, Alisher Navoi and Husayn Boyqaro in Herat, Layla and Majnun, Saddi Iskandariy, Hayratul Abror, Alisher Navoi in Samarkand.

INTRODUCTION

In the years of independence, greater attention has been paid to applying the history of our country based on written sources. The study and promotion of the cultural and spiritual heritage created by our ancestors in the distant past have become urgent issues. The long-forgotten names of our ancestors who made significant contributions to the development of science and culture have been revived. During the Soviet era, artists worked within the framework of socialist realism, but now they confidently create works at a high artistic level in various movements and themes, including avant-garde, romanticism, impressionism, abstractionism, and others, that interest them.

MAIN BODY

After many years of exploration, artist Sa'dulla Abdullayev, in the years of independence, returns to the early stages of his creative work and once again turns to the artistic heritage of medieval Eastern art. He begins to create remarkable and distinctive works on various historical themes. The figures in Abdullayev's works might seem outwardly distinct from one another, but as seen in his piece The Poets of Kokand, it is not movement but rather a deep contemplation, a reflection of dreams and desires, that unites them. This unity has a special musical quality. The uniqueness of the figures in his works arises from comparing elements like their forms, positions, gestures, and movements. Therefore, every line created by his hand carries its own unique meaning. In Abdullayev's works, the line is always used purposefully. The lines that express the human form convey fluidity, harmony, and softness in the artist's works. In the artist's creative process, the life and activities of Alisher Navoi define the essence of his creative reality. Throughout his artistic journey, Abdullayev continually improves in his creative work on historical paintings, producing masterpieces with enthusiasm and inspiration. Among the artist's works created over the years, based on the immortal works of Navoi and related to his state affairs, are paintings such as Layla and Majnun, Saddi Iskandariy, Hayratul Abror, Alisher Navoi and Husayn Bayqaro, Farewell to Samarkand, and Alisher Navoi in Samarkand.

S. Abdullayev's 1991 painting

"Alisher Navoi and Husayn Bayqaro in Herat" is considered one of the best works created in the historical genre in Uzbek visual art at the end of the 20th century and the beginning of the 21st century. The artwork, measuring 1.50 by 2 meters, was created using oil paints on canvas. The idea behind this piece was inspired by the fact that 1991 was declared the Year of Alisher Navoi, which is why the artist chose to create this painting. The composition is horizontal and executed in the style of symbolism. The artist used mannerism to depict the characters in an idealized form. S. Abdullayev used bright colors to reveal the characters of Navoi and Husayn Bayqaro. He portrayed Navoi in green, symbolizing his poetic nature, and Husayn Bayqaro in yellow, representing the symbol of royalty. The bright and localized color usage indicates that the painting was created in the Decorative Art style. The culture of Herat's garden parks is well-

thoughts, holding a prayer beads and the Quran. In the later years of his life, Yasawi intentionally withdrew to a subterranean chamber built at his request, where he lived and created in the light of a candle.

During these years (1991-1992), the artist also created works related to Alisher Navoi's life, such as *"Alisher Navoi in Samarkand"* (1992) and *"Farewell to Samarkand"* (1991). Another of the artist's compositions related to Alisher Navoi was created in 1995. This work, in the form of a diptych, is titled *"The Uzbek Renaissance: Navoi and Jami"* by the artist.

Historical literature provides numerous accounts of the strong friendship and master-disciple relationship between Jami and Navoi. Jami first met Alisher Navoi during the reign of Timurids under Sultan Abu Said, in the area of Khiyabon, where Jami presented one of his works. In 1476-1477, Navoi recognized Jami as his spiritual guide. Despite Jami being older than Navoi and formally considered the master, in essence, they were true friends and collaborators. Jami mentions Navoi with respect in several of his works, such as *"Nafaxtoluns"* and *"Bahariston"*, and Navoi reciprocates in his own writings, including *"Khamzat ul-Muttahayyirin"* and other works.

Abdullayev's high-quality images and his striving for masterful forms are closely linked to the themes and selection of characters he chooses. The artist, in turn, turns to the era of Amir Temur and the Timurids, creating skillful epic works like "Amir Temur is Granting the Victory" and "The Baburids in India". He also created the large triptych "The Uzbek Renaissance" between 1997 and 1999. This piece is one of the artist's perfect works in this genre, resulting from years of research and effort. In the first canvas, the artist created a festive and celebratory mood that captures the victorious moments of Amir Temur.

Historical sources mention that "Amir Temur, while continuing the traditions that existed in Movaraunnahr, celebrated each of his victories with festivals and feasts, honoring every dear guest with a banquet and a celebration."

The aspect the artist focused on was capturing the moment when Amir Temur returned to his homeland after a victory. The scene shows Amir Temur entering the city with his military forces, accompanied by the sounds of trumpets and horns. In front of him, two horn players on horseback are playing, while in the center, Temur rides his white-gray horse in festive attire. The nobles of the land are depicted with arms raised in prayer to welcome him, while Temur's trusted companions, assistants, and military cavalry, holding lances and flags, are shown beside and behind him. The artist paid particular attention to detail, as seen in the depiction of the "white flag." In Amir Temur's battles, the flags held special meaning. The triangular flag, raised high by his army, depicted three circles and symbolized his victory. Although Amir Temur's flag has not survived, there are some references to it in the chronicles and written sources from that time. According to Klavihon, ... (text seems to continue further). In the depiction of Temur, three circles are shown, symbolizing that he was the ruler of three parts of the world." With this, the artist highlights, with a single element, how great a warrior Sahibqiron (Amir Temur) was. In terms of the composition, it also recalls the Renaissance of medieval Europe. However, in the general spirit of the era, one can feel the characteristic color palette and atmosphere of the East. Another important aspect of the painting is that through the artwork, the viewer can vividly feel the true reflection of great history.

In the second painting, the artist emphasizes Amir Temur's focus on architecture. According to the artist, the capital of the great Temurid state, Samarkand, was to become the most beautiful city on Earth. To achieve this goal, the great ruler employed all of his resources. For many years, Samarkand remained the most inspiring architectural source in the world and the central hub of culture and art in Central and Western Asia. Leading architects and builders from conquered countries were brought here, which contributed to the emergence of a new direction in world architecture. This passage elaborates on the symbolic elements in the painting, linking them to the grandeur of Amir Temur's reign, his emphasis on architectural achievements, and his vision of Samarkand as a cultural and architectural epicenter.

    In the painting, the artist depicts Amir Temur during the construction of the Temur Jome Mosque and the Saroymulk Khanim Madrasa, after returning from his campaign to India on May 11, 1399. The ruler had set a goal to build a mosque that would become a symbol of all the mosques in the Muslim East. He brought in architects from Central Asia, Iran, and India to oversee the construction of this large building and provided them with his instructions. All the rulers are listening attentively to his words. At the same time, the ongoing construction is depicted in the background of the composition, where we can see the construction taking place. This passage highlights the historical context of Amir Temur's architectural ambitions and his involvement in overseeing the construction of monumental buildings, as well as how the artist captured this moment in time, emphasizing the significance of the mosque and madrasa in the ruler's legacy.

The main square of the Timurids in Samarkand began to take shape during Ulugh Beg's reign. After Amir Temur's death, the struggle for the throne among the

Timurids intensified, and attention to the development of science, culture, and art began to wane. However, Mirzo Ulugh Beg, even during such a turbulent period, continued the great works started by his grandfather, with a particular focus on the advancement of science. This is why the artist depicted his image in the third part of the triptych. In the painting, Mirzo Ulugh Beg is shown between 1424 and 1428, leaving the observatory he had built near the Obirahmat region of Samarkand, accompanied by two of his scholars. Ulugh Beg is depicted speaking animatedly, with his hands raised toward the sky, suggesting that his favorite topic of conversation was the study of the stars.

This passage highlights the importance of Ulugh Beg in continuing the intellectual and scientific legacy of the Timurids and shows how the artist captures a moment in history where Ulugh Beg is deeply engaged in scholarly discussion, reflecting his passion for astronomy. Although Ulugh Beg is depicted in royal attire, it can be felt that the artist made an effort to portray him more as a scholar than a ruler. One of the companions next to him is a scholar holding several books in his hands, listening attentively to Mirzo Ulugh Beg's words. Similarly, a young student of knowledge is depicted beside him. When portraying the characters, the artist avoids exaggeration and strives to reflect them in a realistic and life-like manner.

The overall essence of the painting is created by the depiction of the observatory behind the characters. This view of the observatory is based on historical sources, as the building itself has survived only in a small portion until our time. In general, before creating this canvas, Sa'dulla Abdullayev placed great importance on ensuring its life-like and accurate portrayal. He thoroughly reviewed numerous materials, forming a true image of the era in his mind, and only after that did he translate this vision onto the canvas. This passage emphasizes how the artist strived to depict Ulugh Beg as a scholar and intellectual, and how careful research and historical accuracy were central to creating an authentic representation of the time and place.

The artist's "The Baburids in India" (2005) is directly related to this historical event. In this work, Babur is depicted not as an invader of India, but rather, first and foremost, as a ruler focused on consolidating state power. He aimed to unite the fragmented land, which was divided into small feudal kingdoms and principalities, into a unified state. He worked to bring the regions of the country together under a central authority, achieving significant results in this regard. At the same time, as a statesman and a military leader who spent much of his life in battle, Babur found time for creative pursuits even during the most challenging and dangerous periods of his personal life and reign. He gathered intellectuals, artists, and creators around him, supported them, and encouraged their work. In the center of the triptych, the artist portrays Babur hosting a peaceful gathering with artists and scholars.

In the miniatures of the "Baburnama", there is much information about the banquets held in Babur's honor in gardens. One such garden was the "Bagh-i-Jahan-Ara" (The Garden of the World). The artist, too, depicts one of these banquets held in honor of Mirzo Babur. This passage highlights how the artist captures Babur's dual nature as both a warrior and a patron of art, showcasing his efforts to unite his kingdom while also fostering a rich cultural and intellectual environment. The scene of the banquet serves as a reflection of Babur's support for the arts and scholars. In the scene, Mirzo Babur is depicted at the center, surrounded by scholars, musicians, and his close companions, all dressed in Eastern attire. In the miniatures, the primary character – Babur, along with his prominent courtiers, is allocated a central place, while secondary figures and officials are positioned according to etiquette and social hierarchy. The people and additional elements are arranged in a harmonious manner, with each figure occupying its designated place within the composition.

Babur's central position, seated in the painting, follows the traditions of miniature art, where his distinctive attire, decorations, and the surrounding objects are depicted in a way befitting a king or an emperor. The artist, taking these aspects into account, portrays Babur in a royal manner. He wears a medium-sized turban adorned with precious decorations, and a long red robe without sleeves, inside a sleeveless, flowing cloak. Babur is seated on a higher throne compared to the others, symbolizing his higher status. The other figures are also depicted in Eastern-style clothing, with none of them wearing attire typical of Indian culture. This is because Babur gathered intellectuals and dignitaries from Mawarannahr around him. This passage highlights how the artist captures the royal nature of Babur and his court, adhering to traditional conventions of representation in miniature art, while also emphasizing the cultural and intellectual environment Babur cultivated around him. The absence of Indian-style clothing among his entourage reflects the Central Asian and Timurid influence on his court.

On the left side of the triptych, Shoh Jahon, the last representative of the Baburid dynasty, is depicted with his daughter, Jahon Oro Begim. This representation highlights Shoh Jahon's efforts to restore and reunite the large empire that the Baburids had created but which was falling apart during his reign. Additionally, he stands out among other princes as a patron of art and culture. Jahon Oro Begim, the beloved daughter of Shoh Jahon, took on the responsibility of managing the royal household after the death of her mother, Mumtoz Mahal. She also assisted her father in governance, internal and foreign policy, and diplomacy by providing him with valuable advice. Like her great-grandfather Babur Shah, she had a great interest in architecture and urban development.

The artist portrays the two figures, despite the historical gap between them, almost as participants in the same central event. Shoh Jahon is depicted in traditional Indian attire, looking towards the center, while Jahon Oro Begim, in a red elegant gown, places her hands on her chest in a respectful gesture. The artist, recognizing their historical significance, chooses to portray them together, suggesting that they followed a similar path to that of their ancestors, perhaps signaling the continuity of their legacy. This is symbolized by the setting of their figures on a path that seems to stretch towards infinity. On the right side of the center, Zebuniso Begim is depicted with her attendants.

Zebuniso stands with her hands folded, listening intently to an attendant who is reading aloud from a book in the soft light of a lamp. Historically, Zebuniso Begim was known as an enlightened woman, demonstrating her intellectual and cultural contributions. This passage illustrates the interconnectedness of the figures in the artwork, highlighting their roles in the continuity of the Baburid legacy and their contributions to culture, governance, and intellectual pursuits. The artist skillfully places these historical figures within a symbolic space, emphasizing their influence and importance.

The three parts of the triptych are skillfully connected by the artist. Through this connection, the artist has created an overall representation of the Baburid dynasty. The central figure of Babur is surrounded by the bright figures of his descendants, signaling that the Baburids not only formed a state in India but also built a great culture. This historical fact is expressed in a way that at first glance may seem like a simple event, but upon closer inspection, it is shown to be deeply rooted in historical significance.

In 2007, the artist created a painting titled "Zebuniso with her disciples," dedicated to the Temurids' princesses. The central figure in the painting is Zebuniso Begim, the daughter of Abu Zafar Muhiyiddin Muhammad Aurangzeb Alamgir, one of the descendants of Zahiriddin Muhammad Babur. Zebuniso Begim was born in February 1639 in Delhi. She was one of the virtuous women of her time, noted for her literacy under the guidance of Hafiza Mariyam Bonu. Her father, recognizing Zebuniso's poetic talent, appointed two prominent scholars of the time, Mulla Muhammad Ashraf Isfahani and Mulla Jovon, as her teachers. Zebuniso Begim became a powerful poet, a distinguished scholar, a master tambur player, and a skilled calligrapher.

She mastered the morphology and syntax of the Arabic-Persian languages, as well as jurisprudence (fiqh), logic, history, and philosophy. She was highly skilled in writing Nastaliq, Nasx, and Shikasta scripts. Zebuniso Begim supported scholars, poets, and artists, paying them salaries and patronizing their work. The words from the "Olami Islam" tazkira confirm this: "Zebuniso Begim earned fame not through her father's rule but through knowledge and ethics." This passage highlights Zebuniso Begim's exceptional qualities, not only as a cultural figure but also as a patron of the arts and scholarship, and emphasizes her intellectual and artistic contributions to her time.

Zebuniso Begim nurtured a number of special disciples, guiding them in the fields of knowledge, ethics, and poetry. The famous Eastern poet, Mirzo Abduqodir Bedil, entrusted his daughter to Zebuniso Begim's care. As a result, she developed into a distinguished poet herself. The artist focuses specifically on this aspect of Zebuniso Begim's character. In the artwork, Zebuniso Begim is depicted sitting with four of her disciples in a garden, engaging in open, free-flowing conversation. She is wearing a long purple dress, with a delicately crafted necklace around her neck, and holding a book she has just read to her disciples. The scene suggests that she is attentively listening to the thoughts and reflections of her young disciples, who are still in the process of discovering life. The disciples, each with different psychological characteristics, are portrayed in various postures. One girl, holding a tanbur with one hand, rests her arm on a tree, deep in thought, while another, standing upright beside her, holds a book in one hand and gazes at her teacher with admiration. On the left of Zebuniso Begim, two other disciples are quietly maintaining decorum, reflecting the importance of discipline and respect in the atmosphere.

In the background, the artist has portrayed the palace built by the Baburids in Delhi, symbolizing the grandeur and cultural richness of the era. This detail highlights that not only men but also women in this dynasty lived with honor, respect, and freedom. Although no direct conversation or debate is taking place among the figures, their gestures and expressions convey a distinct Eastern atmosphere, evoking the spirit of learning and reflection that permeated the environment. Through this composition, the artist emphasizes the intellectual and cultural environment that Zebuniso Begim fostered, as well as the role of women in the flourishing of knowledge and art during the era.

CONCLUSION

Sa'dulla Abdullayev's works in the historical genre hold a unique place in Uzbek painting, with masterpieces such as "Kokand Poets," "Layla and Majnun," "Saddi Iskandariy," "Hayratul Abror," "Alisher Navoi and Husayn Bayqaro," and "The Mughals in India," which serve to immortalize the memories of the Timurids and our great ancestors. In his works, the artistic tool of Mannerism reveals the characters of the figures. Therefore, his creative legacy is crucial for preserving and developing national values, as well as for the recognition of Uzbek art on the international stage.

REFERENCES

1. Kultashev, B., Sadikova, S., & Kultasheva, N. (2021). Development of portrait of Uzbekistan during the early 20th century. *Melbrun. Australia. Swinburne University of Technology.–2021.*
2. Алимкулова Д. 1920–1930-йиллар рангтасвири Ўзбекистон тасвирий санъатининг ривожланиш жараёни кесимида// Санъатшунослик фанлари бўйича фалсафа доктори (PhD) диссертацияси автореферати. – 2020.
3. Лаковская В Л. Послевоенная живопие Узбекистана. Ташкент, 1991 С 88.
4. Юнусхужаева Азиза Саъдулла Абдуллаев ижодида замон талқини. Тошкент. 2022 С 30
4. Khayitboboeva KPA Study Of The Problems Of Tradition And Innovation In Modern Uzbek Folk Art The American

Journal of Social Science and Education Innovations -2021-T3-№ 11-C 14-20

5. Xakimov A.A, Xayitboboyeva X.P. Badiiy tanqid tarixi va nazariyasi. O'quv q o'llanma/ T.:"D iM al" nashriyoti - 2024. - 148bet.

https://lib.cspu.uz/index.php?newsid=1166 9

6. Bokiyeva Guzal Ilhomovna. "O'zbekiston rangtasvirida Sa'dulla Abdullayev ijodining o'rni". Journal of international scientific research Volume 2, Issue 1, January, 2025

CONTENTS

Kamalova Kadriya Fyodorovna
INTERFERENCE OF NATIVE LANGUAGE IN RUSSIAN SPEECH OF STUDENTS – LINGUISTS
...4

Zohira Akhatova Daughter of Akhtam
INTERPRETATION OF HISTORICAL THEMES IN THE WORKS OF ARTIST SADULLA ABDULLAYEV
...20

www.ingramcontent.com/pod-product-compliance
Lightning Source LLC
LaVergne TN
LVHW010437070526
838199LV00066B/6063